# RAISING A VILLAGE: BUILDING AN EMPIRE

## COUPLES CURRICULUM

RHASHEED GAVIN

DR. ALICIA DELGADO-GAVIN

Rhasheed Gavin & Dr. Alicia Delgado-Gavin
Raising a Village: Building an Empire



Published by Spines
ISBN: 979-8-89383-403-1

*There are no instructions on being a parent. When God blesses you with children, parents don't understand how our world changes forever. My husband and I have had the privilege of raising four beautiful children. This curriculum is dedicated to our children. You have taught us so much. We would like to thank you, Alayah, LJ, Talia, and RJ. You are truly our inspiration.*

# CONTENTS


PART I
Keeping Our Relationship and Business
Rooted in God      1

PART II
Transitional Mindset from Bachelor to
Husband and Girlfriend to Wife      5

PART III
Loving Your Spouse More than Your
Selfishness      9

PART IV
Compromising One's Decisions; Knowing
When to Lead and When to Follow      13

PART V
Keeping it Real vs. Being Mindful      17

PART VI
The Blame Game Never Works Unless You
are Blaming Yourself      19

PART VII
Responding vs. Reacting; Choosing
Humbleness over Pettiness      23

PART VIII
Breaking Through Breakdowns      27

PART IX
Breaking Through Breakdowns      29

PART X
Navigating Through Financial Hardships      31

PART ELEVEN

**DISSOCIATIVE LOVE: WHEN YOU
ENGAGE IN OTHER THINGS RATHER
THAN YOUR SPOUSE NEEDS**

When people fall out of love    35

How do you maintain a successful
marriage and relationship?    37

Personal Time: A person must recollect
and reconnect    39

Personal goals and family values    41

Vacations are essential to mental wellness    43

Love from intention instead of present    45


PART XII

Breaking Generational Curses    47

PART XIII

Challenging Social Myths    51

# PART ONE
# KEEPING OUR RELATIONSHIP AND BUSINESS ROOTED IN GOD

God's word is filled with valuable insights, no matter how good our plan, we still need God's help if we are going to succeed.

2 SAMUEL 10:11-12

My wife and I were raised knowing God, as well as both, being familiar with the Bible and its teachings. Although knowing God was an integral part of our lives, we did not realize how vital and essential it was to include God first in every and any decision we needed to make in our marriage, as well as in our business. We made a conscious effort to learn from others' mistakes. Instead of acting like "know it all's", we constantly humbled ourselves and frequently counseled

God through prayer. Both of us grew up in homes where our parents were not married and had children at a young age. Other than television, we had very few examples to pull from regarding maintaining and enjoying a happy marriage, let alone a functioning business.

Let's not get it twisted, we struggled like any other couple. Trust, infidelity, poor money management, and a multitude of trials and tribulations seemed to never end. I often asked myself, how can I love someone so much and it not be enough to ensure happiness and wellness together? Major and minor setbacks made us realize that God was in control, regardless of our intentions and dreams.

I would consider my husband to be more of a "realist" or a logical person, as we would call it, and I am the dreamer. I always had big dreams and set major goals for myself. Ones that most would say are unattainable and even unrealistic. Regardless of our many setbacks, something in me knew to never settle. To not let what others thought or said stop me from pursuing my dreams. I knew that if I had God on my side, nothing could stop me. Not until one day, when my faith was tested beyond belief, did I not truly understand God's power.

In 2016, my husband and I faced some life-altering trials, and looking back, we have no idea how we got through it. I had just had my third child; we had both lost our jobs and were facing eviction. I was at the point where I could not even utter a word of prayer. I was numb. One night, while my husband and I were sitting in our bed, we asked, how did we get to this place? We were despondent and downtrodden. As the tears rolled down our cheeks, all we could do was hold each other and start to pray. At that moment, a strong sense of peace filled my body. Within the next few days, we found a place to live. This was the moment we began getting our lives back on track.

From that moment on, we made a constant effort to pray about everything and make sure that our next steps were aligned with God's will for us, not with our desires and earthly wants. That is a very hard thing to do, especially when we must be patient and live on faith, not by sight alone. As this was our daily practice, we realized that every time we consulted with each other and prayed to God about something, if it was for us, it felt right in our spirits. When we tried to take matters into our own hands, things fell apart. My husband and I have both made poor business and personal decisions. We did not pray and ask God for his divine guidance, and we rushed to do what we wanted to do. That led to many disagreements, arguments, and financial strain. After many times falling, we finally learned to let Go and Let God take full control over our lives.

**Lesson:** Life happens without warning; nobody is perfect, and we all make mistakes. God is perfect and he allows certain things to happen so that we can learn from them.

**Tip:** Make sure to keep faith in God and you will always be able to weather the storm.

# PART TWO
# TRANSITIONAL MINDSET FROM BACHELOR TO HUSBAND AND GIRLFRIEND TO WIFE

But from the beginning of creation, 'God made them male and female', 'Therefore a man shall leave his father and mother and hold fast to his wife, and the two shall become one flesh'. So, they are no longer two, but one flesh. What therefore God has joined together, let no man separate.

MARK 10:6-9

When I was younger, I always knew that I wanted to be a wife someday. Although my parents are not married but have been together since they were 14 years old, I knew what a monogamous relationship looked like. I grew up with both parents in the home and that was normal to me. I could not have it any other way.

My husband was raised by a single mother. When I met him, he was against marriage and made it clear that he loved the bachelor life. At the time, I was just getting out of an abusive relationship, and he was ending a long-term relationship, so essentially, we were both having fun.

As we continued to grow our friendship, we fell in love. Our spirits felt familiar like we had met in another lifetime. Ten years and four children later, we decided to get married. We knew that going into a marriage, we had to change our mindsets and be ready to be a Husband and a Wife, and not just have the title.

I had to learn to put my husband above everything. My husband had to learn to control his temptations by not allowing our wants and desires to destroy our trust in one another. We knew that once we said, "I Do", we were living in a higher purpose together and making a covenant with God to be loyal.

Being a selfish partner in a relationship usually ends in regret and spite. Matters of the heart are often fickle. Feelings come and go as well as temptations, but the thing that fuels the soul and heart is selfless love. The love that will allow you to appreciate your partner even when they are not giving you gifts but you still value their presence. The kind of love that grants you peace and security knowing someone truly loves you beyond your past trauma, appearance, or financial circumstance and overall has your well-being as a priority.

Selflessness in a relationship builds trust, commitment, and reliability. Being selfless creates security and accountability, which serves as a strong foundation to build your lasting relationship. Building a strong and lasting relationship, requires mindfulness, consideration, trust, compassion, and most importantly, God is the rock on which our relationship and foundation are built.

**Lesson:** Letting Go of Lust to Hold on to Love.
**Tip:** Always be transparent with your spouse about your wants, needs, and desires. It does not make you a bad person to feel tempted at times, it makes you human.

# PART THREE
## LOVING YOUR SPOUSE MORE THAN YOUR SELFISHNESS

However, let each one of you love his wife as himself, and let the wife see that she respects her husband.

EPHESIANS 5:25

Loving yourself and promoting your value and self-worth allows your spouse to respect, admire, and honor your worth. Many people don't understand what it truly means to love themselves. People feel that if they look nice, buy expensive things, or just simply do not care what others think about them, then they love themselves. Loving yourself is deeper than that. You can do all those things but still have no respect for yourself. In our marriage, we learned that holding on to anger, regret, and resentment, is a form of not respecting or valuing ourselves. We were allowing those negative seeds to consume us, which in turn was killing us spiritually, mentally, and emotionally.

Holding on to things of the past was selfish on both of our parts and we would justify why we should hold on to these negative feelings. We were holding on to negative things that were connected to our families, friends, past relationships, and things that we may have done or said to each other. These behaviors were toxic and selfish on both of our parts. Before being married, we would use our past hurts against one another, which is wrong.

The moments leading up to our wedding were a true testament to how we needed to love our spouse more than our selfishness. I wanted the perfect dream wedding, at any cost necessary, and my husband wanted to hold on to people he loved, despite their traumatic and toxic bonds. May 25, 2019, our wedding day, was transformational for us. We shed so many tears that day but knew that it was necessary for a successful and happy marriage.

In every lesson, there is a blessing. Letting go of your past tendencies and confronting your toxic behaviors was one of the hardest things we had to do to get married with God's blessing. Regardless of intentions or desires, happiness in a marriage can only thrive with God's authority. The covenant my wife and I formed with God allowed both of us to transform into one. Living to serve God and honor each other; magnifying our talents and abilities, breaking the generational curse off our family, and setting a foundation of spiritual and tangible wealth.

Sure, it was hard to distance myself from my maternal family, but being around them naturally triggers tendencies and behaviors of comfort and familiarity, but they also trigger toxic behaviors as well.

For me to learn and grow into a husband and father I need to protect my family and positively cultivate their development, I gladly separate myself from that toxic bond to focus solely on my family. That's the blessing I chose from this lesson.

**Lesson:** People are afraid to let go of their selfish wants and desires, not realizing that it is necessary for future happiness and development.

**Tip:** Make sure to focus your energy on your marriage and it will become enjoyable.

# PART FOUR
## COMPROMISING ONE'S DECISIONS; KNOWING WHEN TO LEAD AND WHEN TO FOLLOW

Not so with you. Instead, whoever wants to become great among you must be your servant.

MATTHEW 20:26

Compromising is one of the hardest things to do in any relationship. Everyone wants to be right, and no one wants to feel as though they are losing a part of themselves for someone else. A strong and healthy relationship does not only entail compromise but knowing when to lead and when to follow. Instinctually, men want to lead. Society has deemed men being the head of the household and women following the man with everything, as the social norm. In today's age, the roles have shifted. More women are the breadwinners, and more men are stay-at-home dads. There is nothing wrong with this dynamic. The issues arise when mutual interests are not met.

This has been a major characteristic of our relationship. When we met, we were both working and taking care of our business. While I was in school completing my doctorate, my husband took care of the children and worked to take care of the bills. Then, like most unforeseen things in life, my husband lost his job right before the birth of our third child. We were in an extremely tough spot. Not only were finances the number one issue in our relationship, but we both struggled with compromising and trusting the other to make sound decisions.

As we worked through these tumultuous times, we learned that listening was important and that if both parties don't benefit from the decision, then most likely, it's not the right decision. With every decision, you should weigh the pros and cons and then pray about it.

Coming to a mutual understanding is imperative to have a strong, supportive, relationship. Compromising maintains balance and respect. It allows your partner to be invested in the decision-making process and alleviates "the sense of being taken advantage of" or "being forced into decisions without any input". Listening to and understanding your partner quells future fights and disagreements. Having a shared understanding and comprehensive communication puts both parties on the same page, enabling the couple to make sound and wise decisions together.

Communication and shared understanding equals power couple. There is power in compromise.

**Lesson:** Great leaders are supportive followers.
**Tip:** Work on listening more and talking less. That way both parties will be able to learn from one another.

# PART FIVE
# KEEPING IT REAL VS. BEING MINDFUL

A fool vents all his feelings, but a wise man holds them back.

PROVERBS 29:11

It is very difficult to pacify your anger fueled by frustration when it comes to relationships. People often insist on getting the truth, but very few can handle the truth without responding negatively. Sure, you want to be open and transparent with your partner, but confronting an uncomfortable truth requires a great deal of mindfulness.

The truth can trigger a range of emotions such as insecurities to blatant disrespect. The concept of "keeping it real" is confronting a loved one with the truth while trying to communicate effectively without belittling them. This form of communication must be done with tact and careful consideration of the other person's feelings. Keeping it real can be toxic if not coupled with mindful practices. You have to ask yourself if venting your feelings and frustrations is worth the negative impact that it can have on your relationship. Ask yourself, how many arguments could have been avoided if both parties applied mindfulness?

Words do hurt and can harm someone's esteem. We must take accountability for our words to ensure that we don't say something that we regret that we cannot take back. There must be a common ground of respect for one another. You can vent constructively, which means making your point with a purpose, not to hurt or prove the other person wrong. While expressing your concerns with one another, keep in mind the love you have and the purpose for being in your partner's life.

**Lesson**: Your words are powerful and they can kill or give life to your relationship.
**Tips**: Work on meaningful communication daily.

Be mindful of one another, even in times of anger.
Say what you mean and mean what you say without saying it in a mean way.
Work on venting without degrading the other person.

## PART SIX
# THE BLAME GAME NEVER WORKS UNLESS YOU ARE BLAMING YOURSELF

Why do you see the speck that is in your brother's eye, but do not notice the log in your eye?

MATTHEW 7:3-5

It is easy to find fault in others but not so easy to see the faults in yourself. No one is perfect but GOD! Being judgmental is second nature to most folks. Pointing out the flaws in others only masks the pain and insecurity that a person harbors inside themselves. A person will release their judgments, vent, and blame their partner for everything that they feel is going wrong. This is known as "dumping", and when this is done by a person that you love and care about, the damage that it causes can be a hefty toll to pay.

It is common for people in marriages and committed relationships to become desensitized to verbal abuse and take the blame for all negative matters. This will cause a person on the receiving end to shut down, which in turn destroys the trust, hope, and peace that is required for a happy and successful marriage.

Remember that the goal is to compromise and work things out. The satisfaction of being right is self-serving, which does not take care of the problem. You cannot change how a person acts or thinks, but you can control your actions and your response to others.

We have often made the mistake of blaming each other when we've made poor decisions, especially when it came to financial matters. The more we argued, no matter who was to blame, we both had to come up with a solution to fix the problem. The blame game hindered us from being able to find productive solutions to any of our problems. We lost sight of our purpose as husband and wife and as parents to our four children. That lack of accountability led to terrible fights and ugly versions of ourselves. We were focused on things that we could not change, rather than focusing on the things that we could.

So how do we work on this detrimental part of our relationship? Openly accepting your role in the dissension and taking responsibility for your actions is a great place to start in repairing a damaged relationship.

**Lesson**: Look at the man in the mirror before you point the finger.

**Tips**: The blame game never fixes the problem.

Reiterate your faults that caused the blame to shut down.
Refocus the energy of blame and anger with support and compassion.

# PART SEVEN

# RESPONDING VS. REACTING; CHOOSING HUMBLENESS OVER PETTINESS

But he gives more grace. Therefore, it says, "God opposes the proud, but gives grace to the humble".

JAMES 4:6

"Being humble is a lifestyle, not a trend"

THE REALIST

You must use grace when handling emotional matters. Grace allows you to get your point across with finesse. It is easy to overreact and respond negatively in many situations and mistakenly assume things rather than communicate facts or details. Communication is key to responding humbly rather than reacting out of misunderstanding. Pettiness is another nature that comes easily to most. Someone being petty stems from ungratefulness.

Many people worry about small and insignificant things to cover up bigger issues. This is where PRIDE plays a major part in disagreements. We can't use our pride to justify hurting others. When we stop focusing on little, petty things and being selfish, God rewards us with big blessings. When a person can put pride aside, they become humble. Humbleness is confidence, strength, and wisdom.

Words have power and when not used correctly, can be very destructive. My wife would always tell me that even though I was in the right, it was my approach and the way I reacted to a situation that made it worse. Learning to be more mindful of my approach enabled my message to be better received. I had to learn how to respond to my wife instead of negatively reacting out of frustration fueled by a petty mindset.

When a conflict arises, self-check where you are emotionally and mentally to ensure that you are in the right mindset to discuss with your partner the current situation. Try not to be lost and overwhelmed in the moment. Always keep in mind that things can get better moving forward. This will allow for any petty feelings and thoughts to dissipate.

**Lesson**: Reaction to feelings usually turns to conflict. Responding to thought usually resolves conflicts.

**Tip**: Try to pause and count to 5 before responding to a person. It will give you time to process what you want to say before reacting to emotion.

# PART EIGHT

# BREAKING THROUGH BREAKDOWNS

I have said these things to you, that in me you may have peace. In the world, you will have tribulation. But take heart; I have overcome the world.

JOHN 16:33

Being in a family with any unseen circumstances, like anything you have your good and your bad days. Finding the balance between overreacting and stonewalling can be a difficult task when you are processing your emotions.

A family unit is a collection of mixed emotions, especially when navigating uncomfortable situations. Using the power of prayer is a common ground. It allows the family to align their emotions and their intentions into a common focus. There is something so calming about prayer. As the Bible teaches, using God as the foundation of any relationship is the cornerstone of building a strong relationship.

Our family has made this mistake more than once. We originally believed that all the conflict we experienced could be handled by our own devices and control. Not until we unified in prayer did, we all become aligned into a common goal and shared respect for one another. Many people believe because they are intelligent or educated that they have all the answers to how to solve a problem in a relationship. But we can assure you that most problems cannot be fixed with intelligence.

By humbling ourselves, we allow God to intervene in our hearts, which produces a natural conflict resolution. We are no longer distracted by emotions flaring, and we can focus on the love that we all share as a family.

**Lesson**: We as humans, do not have all the answers for our trials and tribulations, but God does.

**Tip**: Instead of overreacting to a conflicting situation, simply gather hands and pray. It has done wonders for our family during some of our most difficult times.

# PART NINE
# BREAKING THROUGH BREAKDOWNS

My soul is weary with sorrow; strengthen me according to your word.

PSALM 119:28

Space is something that we all take for granted. Most people don't realize when space for themselves is needed or when they are being energy vampires and sucking the life out of their loved ones. Those sucking the energy out of their spouses don't realize the toll that it is taking on their relationship. People then become frustrated and resentful of their partner. They begin to lash out in many ways that can be damaging to the relationship when a simple conversation is needed to be able to express how overstimulated you are feeling.

Taking time to reflect is imperative in maintaining

your peace. As a couple, we seldom get these moments to ourselves. And because we get so few moments, we usually overreact out of frustration.

When it comes to children, their needs are usually met before the needs of their parents. This takes a toll on the relationship for multiple reasons. Children do not realize or understand that parents need a break unless explained by the parental figures. Children are not mindful of the space and time restraints that parents are under unless taught to be mindful. Constantly bombarding a parent with their needs creates a stressful and hostile temperament within the family structure.

Although the parents must meet their children's needs, they are human and that level of stress becomes detrimental to the well-being of the parental figures.

**Lesson**: Needing space does not make you a bad partner or parent.
**Tip**: Being able to vocalize your needs to your loved ones without feeling guilty

# PART TEN
# NAVIGATING THROUGH FINANCIAL HARDSHIPS

So do not worry, saying, 'What shall we eat?' or 'What shall we drink?' or 'What shall we wear?' For the pagans run after all these things, and your heavenly Father knows that you need them.

MATTHEW 6:31-32

When it comes to finances, it is one of the most complicated matters within any relationship. People have different opinions and perspectives when it comes to spending and handling their financial matters. Finances are the number one cause of divorce. This is one thing that people don't talk about when they start dating. They don't ask questions about finances such as what your credit score is, how much debt you have; what your thoughts and feelings about money are, do you have any money traumas, how the people in your family handle finances, and what is your goal regarding your financial literacy. If people were transparent about these things early in their relationship, then couples would have a better grasp on their finances and the goals that need to be set for the future.

Hiding your finances is one of the most detrimental and deceptive things that you can do in a relationship. Coming to terms with your financial reality is something you must take to God with heartfelt truth. It requires discipline, honesty, and transparency. Many people feel because they have the money, per se, they are the breadwinners or feel entitled to have whatever they desire, does not mean that they should spend money irresponsibly.

**Lesson**: Finances can be extremely divisive in a relationship. Be highly vigilant of how this can impact your plans.
**Tip:** Be real, honest, and transparent about finances, regardless of how you feel.

# PART ELEVEN
# DISSOCIATIVE LOVE: WHEN YOU ENGAGE IN OTHER THINGS RATHER THAN YOUR SPOUSE NEEDS

With all humility and gentleness, with patience, bearing with one another in love, eager to maintain the unity of the Spirit in the bond of peace.

EPHESIANS 4:2-3

With social media and life being a quick-fix society, being easily distracted is very common in most relationships. It is easy to get inundated with being on our electronic devices for hours and not realizing that we are neglecting our loved ones. Not only is social media a distraction, but people get distracted by work, social life, the kids, and focusing on the things that they feel they lack in their lives, not realizing that the need of their spouse is being put on the back burner.

Mindfulness plays a major part in people not getting

their needs met. People are not mindful of the time that is lost when they get complacent with their current situation. People do not focus on the intimate aspect of their relationship, which in turn, makes people feel unwanted and unappreciated.

## WHEN PEOPLE FALL OUT
## OF LOVE

You can love someone and not be in love with them. Once upon a time, we genuinely love the person we are with. But this does not mean that we like them every day. People fall out of love with one another because they allow the distractions of life to consume them and they forget about why they fell in love with their partner in the first place.

# HOW DO YOU MAINTAIN A SUCCESSFUL MARRIAGE AND RELATIONSHIP?

Work at it like anything else. Positive communication is essential. Being open to forgive the person if they have hurt you, even if something still bothers you. Learn to be the best version of yourself and continue to grow and evolve, Be transparent about your wants and desires. Make sure to work on having introspection about yourself and where you fall short in your relationship. And most importantly, pray together frequently and consistently.

# PERSONAL TIME: A PERSON MUST RECOLLECT AND RECONNECT

Personal time is something that many people fail to utilize. We get caught up in the hustle and bustle of everyday life, that we forget to take that time with our partner. I know that many mothers suffer with parent guilt" where they feel guilty for taking extra time for themselves without the children. This is called self-care. Reading a book quietly, getting a massage, or taking a walk alone is ok and essential for your mental health. How can you be a sufficient partner and parent if your well-being is not intact? Make personal time a priority in your life.

# PERSONAL GOALS AND FAMILY VALUES

etting goals and intentions with your partner and children is a great way to form the building blocks of your life. How can the family have structure or direction if goals are not set? Couples should sit down weekly and discuss the goals for the week, next month, next 6 months a year. This ensures that everyone is on the same page and working towards building the family system. Discussing the values that we share and how we want our family to be raised helps families stay in alignment with their purpose and the things they need to do to build a strong foundation.

# VACATIONS ARE ESSENTIAL TO MENTAL WELLNESS

am a firm believer that everyone deserves time away a few times throughout the year. Engaging in date night, spending the night in a hotel, or taking an adult-only vacation is necessary to recollect yourselves and reconnect on a more intimate level. Studies have shown that people who vacation often have a better wellness of life and health. I know the biggest concern for many people is having the finances to travel. There are so many ways that you can travel on a budget. Make a travel account where you take at least $20 from each paycheck and place it aside. Look for discounts and coupons on travel sites. Or take mini vacations to local hotels. That way you are still spending time together with your partner outside of the house.

# LOVE FROM INTENTION INSTEAD OF PRESENT

Couples often experience periods of ups and downs within any relationship. Love sometimes is a fleeting emotion that comes and goes based on the things and intentions that each person experiences within the relationship. For example, a person can have the intention to surprise and pamper their mate but realistically they don't possess the time or resources to make that happen. Being able to love, respect, and honor your mate without these conditional signs of love can be challenging for a person used to receiving this form of love language. Just because you didn't receive it in the present doesn't mean that your partner is not working on presenting it in the future when circumstances are more feasible. If you truly love them, give your partner a chance to provide these gifts in their own time.

# PART TWELVE
## BREAKING GENERATIONAL CURSES

*The LORD is slow to anger, abounding in love and forgiving sin and rebellion. Yet he does not leave the guilty unpunished; he punishes the children for the sin of the parents to the third and fourth generation.'*

*Numbers 14:18*

Generational curses are something that we do not hear about until our adult life. It wasn't until we started seeing toxic patterns and traits in our family and within us, that we began to study the true meaning of 'Generational Curses'.

Our behaviors stem from our upbringing and how we were raised. My husband and I come from very different backgrounds. My parents were sixteen years old when they had me, I was raised by teenagers and a host of grandparents, aunts, uncles, and cousins. My extended family had much trauma and unorthodox behaviors, such as drug use, divorce, financial poverty, physical violence, and incarceration, just to name a few. My husband grew up with a single mother and a father who was absent for a small part of his childhood. He was extremely close to his maternal grandfather, who passed away when he was nine years old. The passing of his grandfather took a major toll on his family dynamics, which would not be realized until his adult life.

As we embarked on this journey in our relationship, we realized that the way we interacted and treated one another was a firsthand by-product of how we were raised. Some of the traits that were passed on to us were good, and many were not so good.

We had to acknowledge these unhealthy behaviors and ask ourselves what we needed to do to break these cycles and what we needed to do to support one another to ensure that we do not pass this on to our children. We had to acknowledge and confront the uncomfortable part of ourselves that we kept dormant in our subconscious for most of our lives. The trauma that our parents faced was never addressed. We had to peel back each layer of our life to get to the root of our issues. We call this the onion method. Each layer brought about more hurt and tears, but once we got to the center of our hurt, we were able to make a conscious effort to combat the hurt and use it as a lesson.

What we learned is that these generational curses

called for a mindset change. We had to look at the bigger picture, which was raising our children in a safe and nurturing environment despite our financial limitations and misguided behavioral traits. We focused on raising our children with a more positive mindset and more open communication. We did not want to continue the toxic cycles that we were told were "normal". We had to not just tell our kids how to heal and love the right way, we had to show them.

**Lesson**: We have no control over the curses and toxic traits that are passed down from generation to generation. But we can be better people to one another and end the curse with us once we understand how to heal.

**Tip**: Healing hurts. Don't be afraid to peel back the layers of hurt to get to the peace you need to have a thriving life.

# PART THIRTEEN
# CHALLENGING SOCIAL MYTHS

*For the time will come when they will not endure sound doctrine; but wanting to have their ears tickled, they will accumulate for themselves teachers in accordance to their desires, and will turn away their ears from the truth and will turn aside to myths.*

*2 Timothy 4:3-4*

As a child, I knew that I always wanted to be a mother and a wife. My husband stated that he always wanted to be a father, but not get married. One myth I had is that once you get married, God will release a multitude of blessings and all the desires of your heart. I am not saying that God is not merciful or a supplier, but I thought of him as a genie. I thought that there would always be great days in marriage; no fighting, steaming hot sex every day, and perfect, well-behaved children. Boy was I wrong.

The trials and tribulations that come with being married and a parent are unmatched. That does not go without saying that if you put GOD at the center and the forefront of your relationship and household, nothing will be too difficult to get through without prayer.

People are not told before being married that you are constantly working every day to be in the relationship. There are moments when you love your partner, but you don't necessarily like them. And that is ok. Being introspective with yourself and your partner is key to unlocking true transparency.

Society today does not value the principles and covenant of marriage. It appears it is designed to distract you with temptation and false expectations for your partner. Divorce has been monetized and has been made a trend on television and social media.

With all these obstacles that couples must face, it is a daunting challenge to remain committed and willing to work on yourself individually and as a pair. We live in a microwave era where everyone wants a quick fix to everything, including the issues in their relationships. More people walk away than fight to build a healthy and lasting relationship. People are encouraged to file for divorce faster than the ink drying on their marriage certificate.

Coming into this relationship we did not know the journey we were about to embark on. We have faced many trials and tribulations, and our faith in GOD and trust in one another have been tested beyond belief. We did not realize that we were just starting our journey of healing as we were falling in love with one another simultaneously. My husband became a stepfather to my two children when they were a toddler and an infant. We've endured medical surgeries and a multitude of financial hardships.

**Lesson**: All of this was necessary to lead us to our purpose and true journey in life.

**Tip**: Remember to put God first in your relationship and every decision, you make

www.ingramcontent.com/pod-product-compliance
Lightning Source LLC
Chambersburg PA
CBHW071511130726
47997CB00006B/2486